C000120852

how2become

KENT TEST BOOKLET

(NON-VERBAL REASONING)

THE
REVISION
SERIES

www.How2Become.com

As part of this product you have also received FREE access to 100s of interactive educational practice papers, including KS2, 11+, KS3 and GCSE test questions.

To gain access, simply go to:

www.MyEducationalTests.co.uk

Get more products for passing any test at:

www.How2Become.com

Orders: Please contact How2Become Ltd, Suite 14, 50 Churchill Square Business Centre, Kings Hill, Kent ME19 4YU.

You can order through Amazon.co.uk under ISBN 978-1-910602-35-5, via the website www.How2Become.com or through Gardners.com.

ISBN: 978-1-910602-35-5

First published in 2015 by How2Become Ltd.

Updated in 2018.

Copyright © 2018 How2Become. All rights reserved.

All rights reserved. Apart from any permitted use under UK copyright law, no part of this publication may be reproduced or transmitted in any form or by any means, electronic or mechanical, including photocopying, recording, or any information, storage or retrieval system, without permission in writing from the publisher or under licence from the Copyright Licensing Agency Limited. Further details of such licenses (for reprographic reproduction) may be obtained from the Copyright Licensing Agency Ltd, Saffron House, 6-10 Kirby Street, London EC1N 8TS.

Typeset for How2Become Ltd by Anton Pshinka.

Disclaimer

Every effort has been made to ensure that the information contained within this guide is accurate at the time of publication. How2Become Ltd is not responsible for anyone failing any part of any selection process as a result of the information contained within this guide. How2Become Ltd and their authors cannot accept any responsibility for any errors or omissions within this guide, however caused. No responsibility for loss or damage occasioned by any person acting, or refraining from action, as a result of the material in this publication can be accepted by How2Become Ltd.

The information within this guide does not represent the views of any third party service or organisation.

CONTENTS

THE
REVISION
SERIES

INTRODUCTION TO YOUR GUIDE

Welcome to your new guide, *11+ Kent Test Non-Verbal Reasoning*. This booklet has been specifically designed with the sole intention of aiding anyone who is taking their Kent Test, by improving their performance during the Non-Verbal section of the exam.

In this guide, we have done our utmost to provide you with preparation and practice tips that will guide you through the process of successfully passing your Non-Verbal Reasoning assessment.

This booklet primarily focuses on the Non-Verbal Reasoning section of the Kent Test. We have also created other testing booklets similar to this one, if you wish to improve your overall performance. If you wish to successfully pass all of the stages of the 11+ assessment, we highly recommend that you take a look at our booklets for English, Maths and Verbal Reasoning.

We wish you the very best of luck in your assessment.

THE
REVISION
SERIES

GENERAL TIPS FOR NON-VERBAL REASONING

GENERAL TIPS FOR NON-VERBAL REASONING

1. Try and visualise the questions!

2. Why not make yourself a cube net as you try to work out the cube-based questions? This will help you to visualise where the shapes on the cube will be positioned once you have folded the cube together.

3. Some people like to work on the questions they find most difficult. Some people prefer to leave the hard questions to the end. Pick a way that you feel comfortable with, and use it throughout your Non-Verbal Reasoning assessments.

4. Accuracy is key! You need to remain as accurate as possible to ensure successful marks. That's why it is important to fully comprehend the questions and understand what is being asked.

5. Try drawing out the questions as you go. Drawing out the answers of what you think it may look like (i.e. if the shape is rotated or reflected etc), will help you to visualise the answers more clearly.

6. Using highlighters is a great way to distinguish your answers. Highlighting is helpful if you are counting lots of shapes or working out numbers or angles etc.

7. When completing grid-based questions, you can always work backwards. By working backwards, you would have to do the opposite to what is being asked. This is a useful way to see if you have the correct answer.

8. Practice is key! If you struggle with visualising shapes and objects, you may struggle with these tests. That is why we have provided you with lots of sample questions for you to work through. The more you practice these tests, the more likely you are to feel comfortable and confident with these types of questions. Remember, practice makes perfect!

9. If you are unsure about the answers, make sure you use our detailed answers and explanations to understand how you get to the correct answer. Remember, knowing where you went wrong is just as important as getting the questions correct. You need to understand how the answer can be reached. Try practising the question again after reading the answers and explanations to ensure you know where you went wrong.

10. Pay attention to everything! If you are unsure about what the differences are, or what is happening in the sequences, pay attention to everything you see. Count all the sides, angles, colours, shading, line types, sizing, rotations, reflections etc. That way you can eliminate what is the same and what is different about the sequence.

11. Check out our free online psychometric testing and sample questions to ensure that you are fully prepared for your Non-Verbal Reasoning tests.

www.MyEducationalTests.co.uk

THE
REVISION
SERIES

EXAMPLE QUESTIONS FOR NON-VERBAL REASONING

Question type 1

Fill in the missing square in order to complete the sequence.

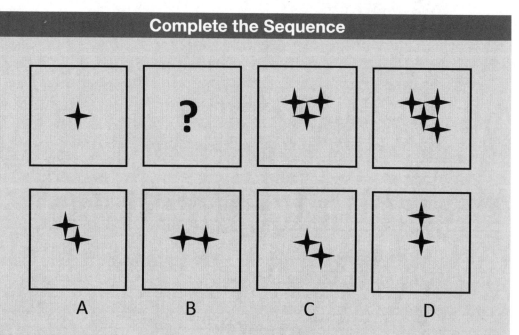

Answer = A

Rule 1 = the sequence adds one diamond each time. The diamond is added from the top left and then continues to be added in a clockwise manner.

In this example, you need to pay particular attention to numbers. The sequence follows the pattern of adding the same shape as the sequence progresses.

In other similar questions, you may need to add or subtract certain numbers of shapes in order for the sequence to be completed.

Question type 2

Which answer option completes the sequence?

Rotating the Figures

Answer = D

Rule 1 = the cross moves one place clockwise.

Rule 2 = the grey dot moves one place clockwise.

Rule 3 = you will also notice that the sequence alternates colours. The big shapes change from black to white. The cross changes from white to black. The dot remains the same colour.

For these types of questions, you need to understand what direction the sequence has been rotated in. Not all the shapes will be rotated in the same direction, so pay attention to what is happening.

Also, you should have noticed that two different patterns are emerging; **rotation** and **alternation**. Some questions may require you to identify more than one pattern in the sequence.

Remember, if you struggle to find the pattern of a sequence, break it down! Take one shape at a time and determine what is happening to that shape as the sequence progresses. Do the same for all of the shapes until you understand everything going on in the patterned sequence.

Question type 3

Which of the answer figures completes the sequence?

Reflections of the Figures

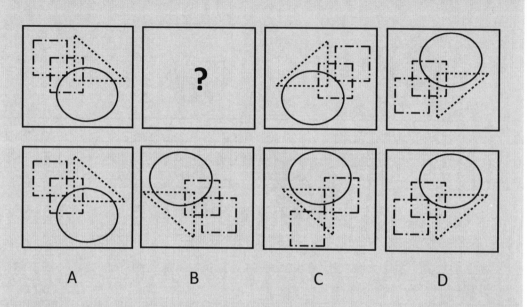

A   B   C   D

Answer = B

Rule 1 = Box 1 and 3 are vertical reflections of one another.

Rule 2 = Box 2 and 4 will be vertical reflections of one another.

For these types of questions, you need to pay attention to what is being reflected.

The reflections may not be seen one after another; they may be reflecting in every other box, or every third box. It is important to look closely at everything that is going on and identify the pattern and similarities of each figure.

Question type 4

Which figure is the odd one out?

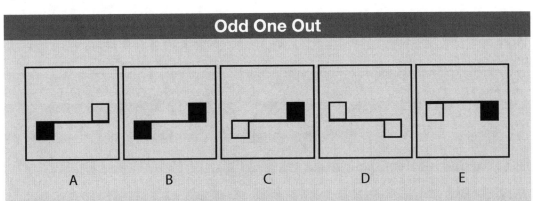

A	B	C	D	E

Answer = E

Rule 1 = the sequence follows the rule of alternation.

Rule 2 = the sequence follows the pattern of one square being on the top of the horizontal line, and one square being on the bottom of the horizontal line.

Figure E is the odd one out because the figure only contains two squares underneath the horizontal line, whereas all of the other diagrams contain one square on top of the line, and one square on the bottom.

For questions like this, you need to pay careful attention to what is changing. You need to distinguish what figure is the 'odd one out' by determining the differences between the figures. This could be based on reflections, rotations, alternations etc.

Question type 5

Which of the cubes can be made from the cube net?

3D Shapes

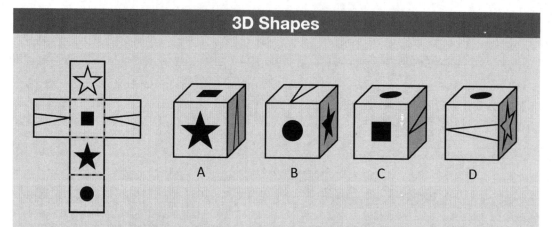

Answer = A

For this type of question, you need to make sure that you fold along the creases of the cube net, so that the shapes remain on the outside of the cube.

Top Tip! If you struggle with these questions, and find it difficult to imagine what the cube would look like, why don't you make a cube using a piece of paper? Make a cube net, draw on the shapes, and see what it looks like!

Given time and practice, these questions will become much easier to visualise in your head. Eventually, you won't have to rely on drawing them out every time!

Question type 6

Which of the Answer Figures fits in with the Question Figures?

Question and Answer Figures

Question Figures

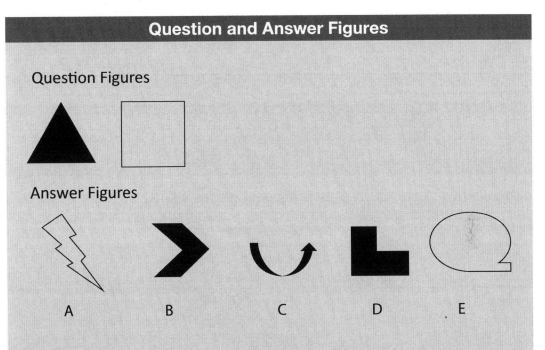

Answer Figures

A   B   C   D   E

Answer = B

Rule 1 = the shape must contain **one or more lines of symmetry.**

For this type of question, you need to pay attention to the Question Figures. What do they show? How are they similar? How can you use these shapes to identify which of the Answer Figures fits in with the same pattern?

Bear in mind that anything can be going on in these questions: rotations, lines of symmetry, numbers, angles, reflections, shapes, sizing etc.

Pay attention to everything and consider the following question carefully: *What makes the Question Figures similar, and what Answer Figure fits in with the same pattern?*

Question type 7

Connect the shapes using the corresponding letters to match up the shapes.

Connecting the Shapes

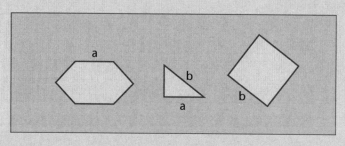

Join all of the 3 shapes together with the corresponding letters to make the following shape:

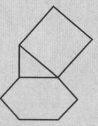

Using the corresponding letters, rotate each shape so that it is positioned correctly with the corresponding letter.

Question type 8

Pointing and counting.

Pointing and Counting

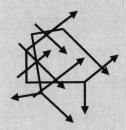

These questions are relatively straightforward, but sometimes it is tricky to count shapes without miscalculating. Be sure to pay attention and do exactly what the question is asking you.

If the question is asking you to count points, you do not need to count all of the lines, just count how many points you can see. If the question asks you to count how many sides the shape has, only count the sides of the shape.

Use a highlighter pen to highlight and count the number of points. That way you won't count the same one twice.

Question type 9

Which test shapes (1, 2 or 3) belong to Set A?

Test Shapes

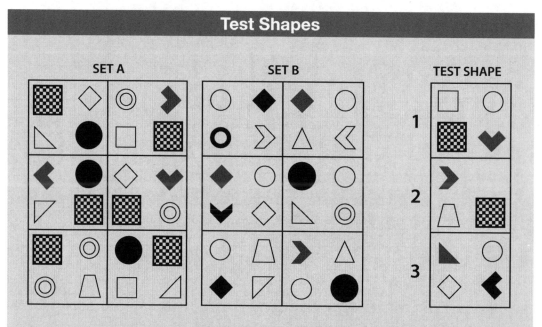

When responding to this type of question we can see that it is the 'issues around the size and shape of objects', the 'number of objects' and the 'shading and colour' that we need to observe and assess in order to reach the correct answers.

Pay attention to what is happening in the sequence.

Question type 10

Determining where the hidden shape is.

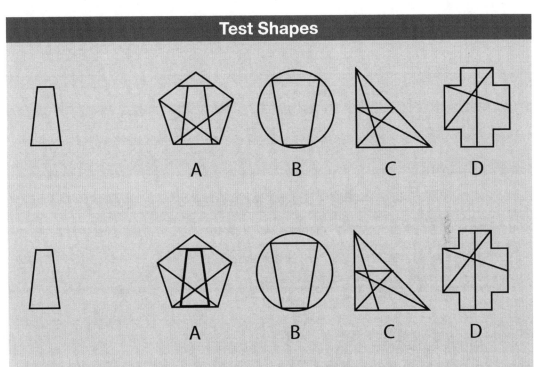

It is important to pay close attention to sizing and positioning. While the shape may look the same, it might not be.

Make sure the hidden shape is the exact same size. Remember, it must remain the same way round where it is hidden.

Answer: A

NON-VERBAL REASONING

(SECTION 1)

Question 1

Which of the Answer Figures fits in with the two Question Figures?

Question Figures

Answer Figures

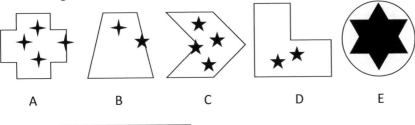

| A | B | C | D | E |

Answer

Question 2

Which figure is the odd one out?

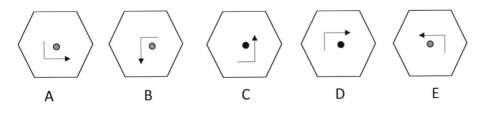

| A | B | C | D | E |

Answer

Question 3

Which figure is the odd one out?

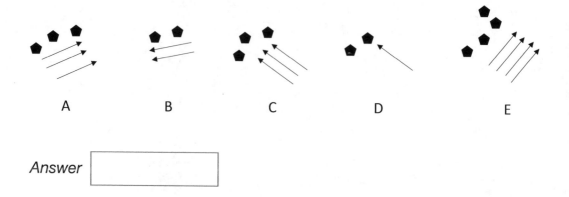

A   B   C   D   E

Answer

Question 4

Work out which of the cubes can be made from the cube net.

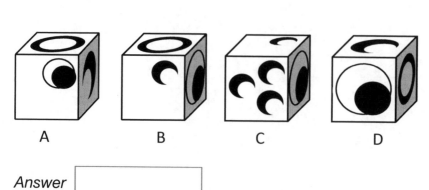

A   B   C   D

Answer

Question 5

Which answer option completes the sequence?

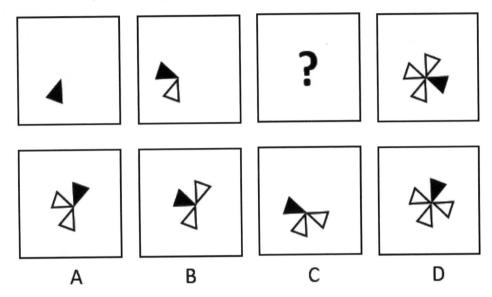

Answer

Question 6

Which answer option completes the sequence?

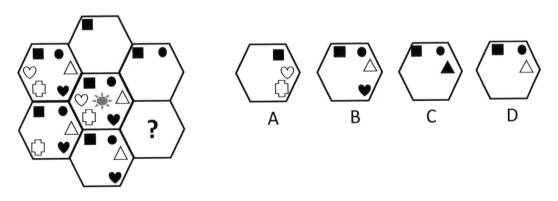

Answer

Question 7

Work out which two shapes are identical. (No rotation or reflection needed). Two answers required.

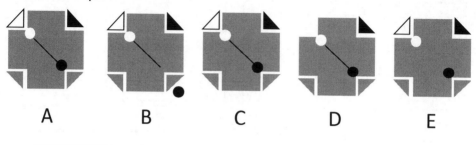

| A | B | C | D | E |

Answer

Question 8

What comes next in the sequence?

A   B   C   D

Answer

Question 9

Work out which figure is the odd one out.

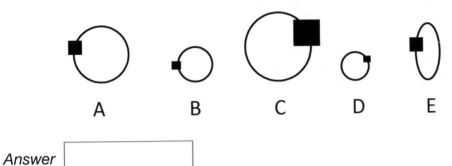

A   B   C   D   E

Answer

Question 10

Complete the pair. Look at how the figure changes from box 1 to box 2, and then apply the same changes in order to find the missing box.

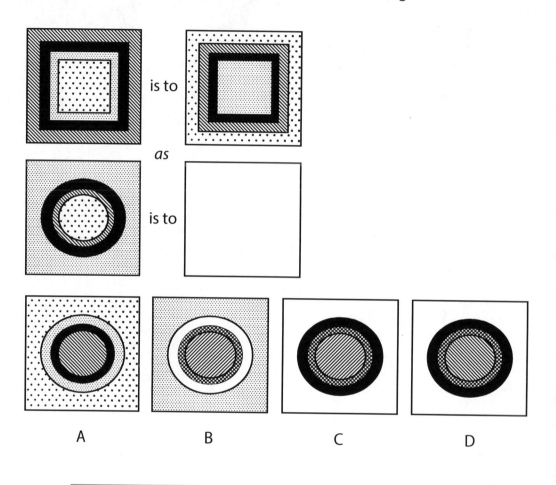

Answer

Question 11

Work out which of the cubes can be made from the cube net.

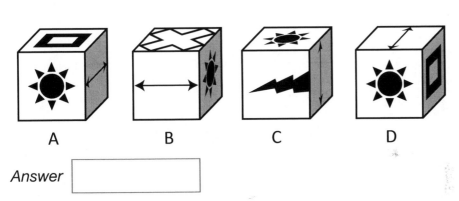

| A | B | C | D |

Answer [   ]

Question 12

Which figure is the odd one out?

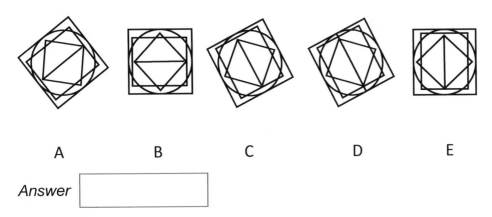

A   B   C   D   E

Answer [   ]

Question 13

Fill in the gap in order to complete the sequence.

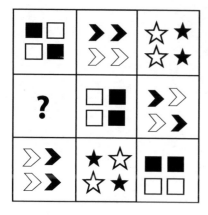

Answer

Question 14

Fill in the gap in order to complete the sequence.

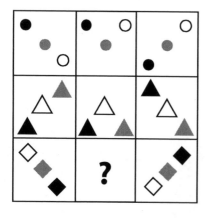

Answer

Question 15

Which figure is the odd one out?

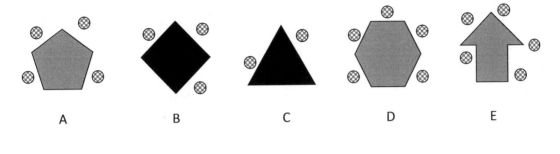

A   B   C   D   E

Answer

Question 16

What comes next in the sequence?

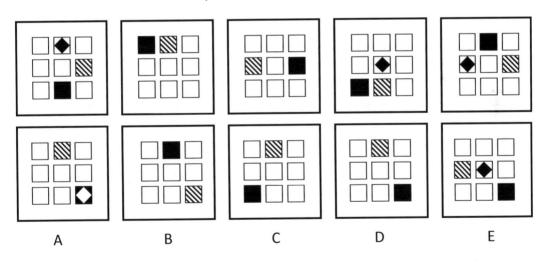

A   B   C   D   E

Answer

Question 17

Which figure completes the sequence pattern?

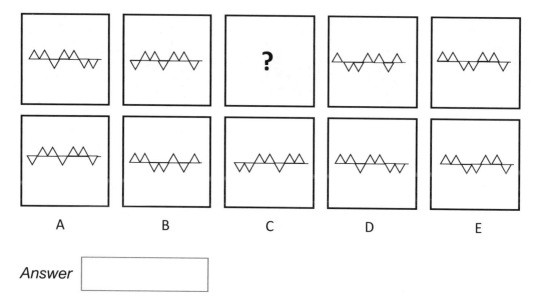

Answer

Question 18

Which figure completes the sequence pattern?

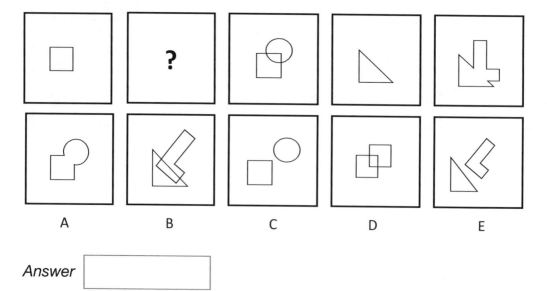

Answer

Question 19

Which figure completes the sequence pattern?

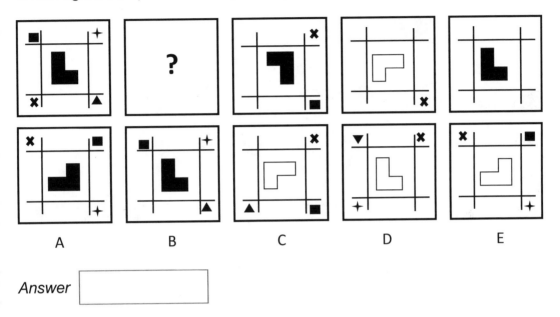

Answer

Question 20

Which figure completes the sequence pattern?

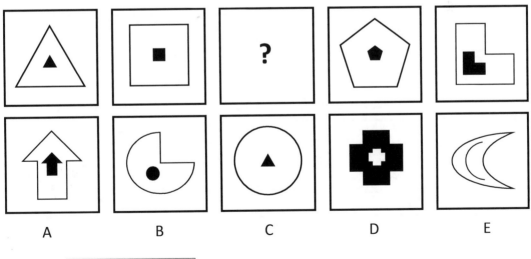

Answer

Question 21

Which figure completes the sequence pattern?

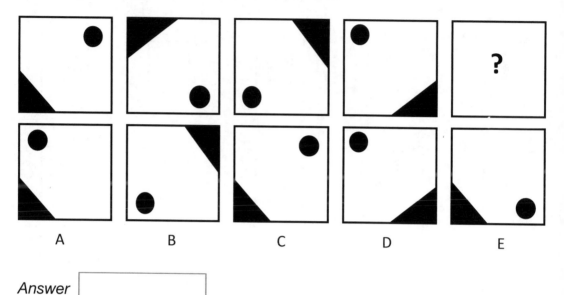

Answer

Question 22

Which figure completes the sequence pattern?

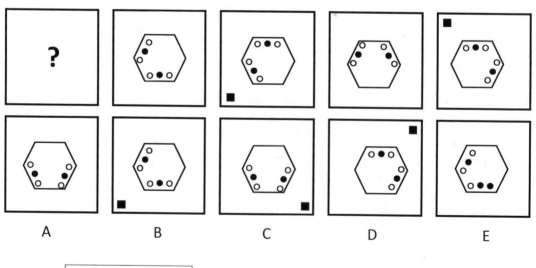

Answer

Question 23

Work out which option (A, B, C or D) would NOT look like the Question Figure if it rotated.

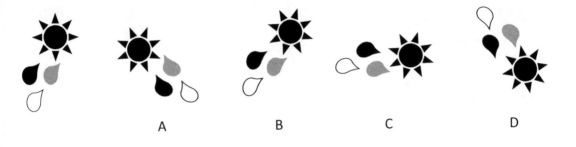

Answer

Question 24

Which figure comes next in the series?

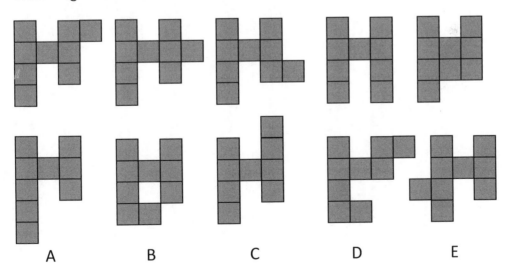

Answer

Question 25

Which figure completes the sequence?

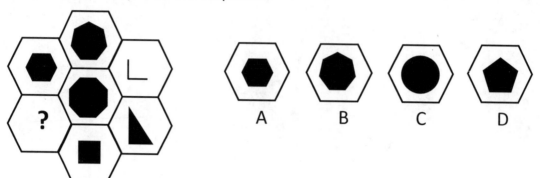

Answer

ANSWERS TO SECTION 1

Q1. C

Rule 1 = all stars in the figure must be five-pointed.

Rule 2 = one of the stars must be overlapping a side of the larger shape.

Figure A can be ruled out because the stars need to be five-pointed, not four-pointed. Figure B can be ruled out because all of the stars need to be five-pointed; one of the stars is only four-pointed. Figure D can be ruled out because none of the stars are overlapping the side of the larger shape. Figure E can be ruled out because the star is a six-pointed star. Also, the star is not overlapping any of the sides of the larger shape.

Q2. D

Rule 1 = the arrow is being rotated (clockwise or anti-clockwise).

Figure D is the odd one out because the arrow has been reflected instead of rotated.

Q3. D

Rule 1 = all the figures contain the same number of arrows as there are pentagons.

Figure D is the odd one out because all of the other figures contain an equal number of arrows as there are pentagons. Whereas in Figure D, there is only one arrow but two pentagons.

Q4. A

Rule 1 = you need to fold along the creases of the cube, so that the shapes are on the outside of the cube.

Figure A is the only cube that shows where each of the shapes would be if you were to build the cube. Figures B, C and D all show the shapes in the wrong position.

Q5. A

The black triangle in tile one moves around clockwise one place whilst one white triangle is added to the right of it.

This makes option A the next tile in the sequence.

Q6. D

Starting from the top hexagon and working in a clockwise manner, ending up in the middle, the pattern follows the sequence of adding one shape to the corner of the hexagon each time. Therefore in the missing hexagon, there needs to be a black square, a black circle and a white triangle.

Q7. A and C

None of the other figures are identical. Figures A and C are identical.

Q8. C

Rule 1 = The white dot starting in the bottom left corner moves two places clockwise, around the edge of the figure.

Rule 2 = The white dot starting second on the first row moves three places clockwise, around the edge of the figure.

Figure A can be ruled out because the white dot third on the first row should be the second dot on the first row. Figure B can be ruled out because the white dot in the bottom right corner should be one place above it; the white dot on the first row should also be moved one place anti-clockwise. Figure D can be ruled out because the white dot on the third row should be the second dot on the first row. Also, the white dot on the second row should be moved one place clockwise.

Q9. E

All of the other figures are circles. Figure E contains a black square (like the others); but instead of containing a circle, it contains an ellipse.

Q10. A

Within the top left-hand square, the different coloured/shaded squares work from the outside towards the centre. Within the top right-hand square, the different coloured/shaded squares work from the centre towards the outside.

Q11. A

Rule 1 = you need to fold along the creases of the cube, so that the shapes are on the outside of the cube.

Figure B can be ruled out because the arrow and the 'cross' sign need to be on opposite sides. Figure C can be ruled out because the 'sun' shape would need to be on the right side of the figure. Figure D can be ruled out because the two-pointed arrow and the square would need to replace one another.

Q12. D

Figure D is the odd one out because all of the other figures are rotations of one another; whereas Figure D has been manipulated. The line going through the middle of the diamond shape has been stretched out and reaches the edge of the square (it should only reach the edge of the diamond shape).

Q13. C

Rule 1 = the shapes move throughout the sequence one space each time. For example, the squares in the first box, on the first row, will be in the second box in the second row, and the third box in the third row.

Rule 2 = the colour pattern moves one space anti-clockwise throughout each row.

Figure A can be ruled out because the stars on the top row should be black, and the stars on the bottom should be white. Figure B can be ruled out because the stars on the top row should be black, not white and black; and the stars on the bottom row should be white, not white and black. Figure D can be ruled out because the stars on the bottom should both be white, not black and white.

Q14. D

Rule 1 = from box 1 to box 2, the shape at the bottom of the diagonal line moves to the top right corner.

Rule 2 = from box 2 to box 3, the shape at the top left corner will move down to the bottom left corner.

Figure A can be ruled out because the white diamond and the grey diamond should be in each other's positions. Figure B can be ruled out because the diamonds should be in the top half of the square, not in the bottom half. Also, the colour pattern of the diamonds is incorrect, from left to right it should be white, grey and black. Figure C can be ruled out because this is a reflection of what the answer should look like.

Q15. E

Rule 1 = the number of dots should be one less than the number of sides on the shape.

Figure E is the odd one out because all of the other figures contain a number of dots that is one less than the number of sides of the larger shape. Figure E has seven sides. Therefore there should be six dots, but there are only five.

Q16. D

Rule 1 = the diamond moves one place from right to left, once it reaches the end of the row, it begins on the right side of the next row.

Rule 2 = the black square moves three spaces around the outer edge in a clockwise motion.

Rule 3 = the diagonal patterned square moves two spaces around the outer edge in an anti-clockwise motion.

Q17. C

Rule 1 = the triangles move one place to the right as the sequence progresses.

Rule 2 = once the triangle reaches the end of the horizontal line, the triangle is placed back at the start.

Figure A can be ruled out because it is a replica of box 2. Figure B can be ruled out because all of the triangles are in the incorrect position. Figure D can be ruled out because it is a replica of box 1. Figure E can be ruled out because it is a replica of box 5.

Q18. A

Rule 1 = to get from box 1 to box 2, the shapes need to merge. It uses one shape (in box 1); and you have to work out which shape it is being merged with (in this case it is a square and a circle). The third box indicates which two shapes have been merged together and demonstrates the overlap.

Rule 3 = after the first three boxes, the sequence begins again, with different shapes; but following the same rule.

Figure B can be ruled out because the shapes merging together need to be a square and a circle. Figure C can be ruled out because the two shapes need to be merged as opposed to separated. Figure D can be ruled out because the two shapes need to be a circle and a square; not two squares. Figure E can be ruled out because the shapes need to be a circle and a square; not a triangle and an 'L' shape.

Q19. E

Rule 1 = the shape in the middle rotates 90° anti-clockwise as the sequence progresses.

Rule 2 = the shape in the middle alternates from black to white as the sequence progresses.

Rule 3 = the small shapes move one position to the next corner (in a clockwise manner).

Rule 4 = as the shapes rotate around, a shape is left off. You will notice, that the 'cross' shape appears the most, therefore this must be the beginning of this sequence, and so the last shape rotated (using the 'cross' to begin) will be left off.

Figure A can be ruled out because the shape in the middle needs to be white, not black. Figure B can be ruled out because the shape in the middle needs to be white, and rotated 90° anti-clockwise. Also, the small shapes do not follow the correct pattern. Figure C can be ruled out because the shape in the middle needs to be rotated 180°. Also the small shapes do not follow the correct pattern. Figure D can be ruled out because the shape in the middle needs to be rotated 90° anti-clockwise. None of the small shapes are in the correct position.

Q20. A

Rule 1 = the large shape is white. The small shape is black.

Rule 2 = the small shape and the large shape are the same shape.

Figure B can be ruled out because the 'pac-man' shape does not contain the same shape in the centre of the shape, it contains a circle instead. Figure C can be ruled out because the large white circle should contain a small black circle, not a black triangle. Figure D can be ruled out because the large shape should be white, and the small shape should be black. Figure E can be ruled out because the moon shape only contains a curved line, not a small moon shape.

Q21. C

Rule 1 = the shapes move 90° clockwise as the sequence progresses.

Figure A can be ruled out because the black dot should be in the top right corner, not the top left. Figure B can be ruled out because the black dot and black triangle should be in one another's place. Figure D can be ruled out because the dot and the triangle need to be moved one corner clockwise. Figure E can be ruled out because the black dot needs to be in the top right corner, not the bottom right.

Q22. C

Rule 1 = the dots move to one side in a clockwise motion.

Rule 2 = every other figure in the sequence contains a black square in the corner of the whole box. This square moves one corner clockwise.

Figure A can be ruled out because the figure does not contain a black square in the bottom right corner. Figure B can be ruled out because the dots are not in the correct position. They need to be positioned so that the side that is empty and in-between the two lines of dots is at the bottom. The black square should be in the bottom right corner, not the bottom left. Figure D can be ruled out because the side that is empty and in-between the two lines of dots should be at the bottom, not on the top right side. The black square should be in the bottom right corner, not the top right. Figure E can be ruled out because the side that is empty and in-between the two lines of dots should be at the bottom, not bottom left. The figure also needs to contain a black square in the bottom right corner.

Q23. D

Figure D is not a rotation of the Question Figure. Figure D is a reflection and then a rotation. Therefore, this is not an exact rotation of the Queston Figure.

Q24. B

Rule 1 = The square starting on the top right (last square on the first row) moves one place around the shape. It circulates the shape in a clockwise manner.

Figure A can be ruled out because the fifth square in the first column should be on the fourth row, second column. Figure C can be ruled out because the first square on the first row, should be on the fifth row, second column. Figure D can be ruled out because the third square on the first row, should be on the third row, third column. Figure E can be ruled out because the square on the third row, first column, should be on the fourth row, third column.

Q25. D

The sequence starts from the top right hexagon (the first one after the top). It follows the pattern of adding one side to the shape before.

For example, a triangle has three sides, so the next figure in the sequence would contain four sides, such as a square. The sequence continues by adding one side to each shape.

THE REVISION SERIES

NON-VERBAL REASONING
(SECTION 2)

Question 1

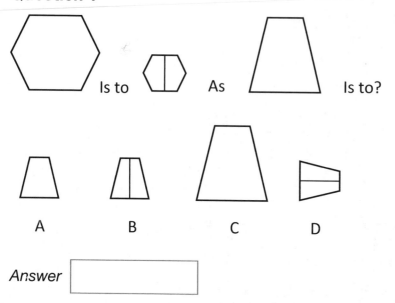

Answer [   ]

Question 2

Which of the following shapes comes next in the series?

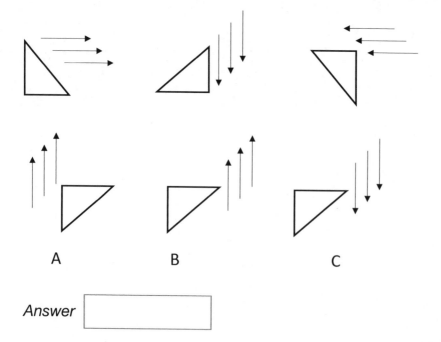

Answer [   ]

Question 3

Which of the following diagrams (A, B or C) comes next in the sequence?

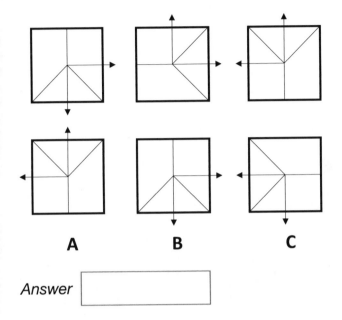

A   B   C

Answer

Question 4

Which of the following diagrams (A, B or C) comes next in the sequence?

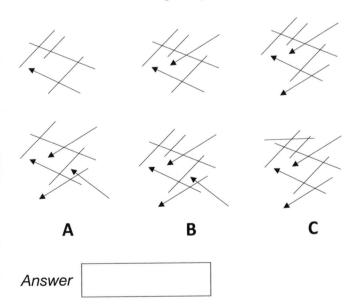

A   B   C

Answer

Question 5

Work out which 3D shapes from the answer figures are needed to create the Question Figure.

Question Figure

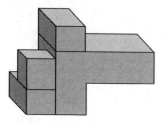

Answer Figures

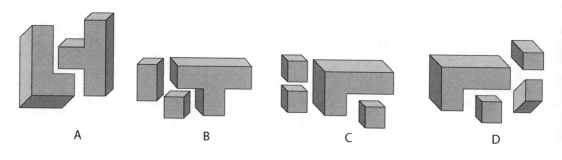

A   B   C   D

Answer

Question 6

Fill in the missing square in order to complete the grid.

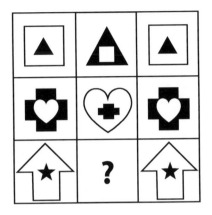

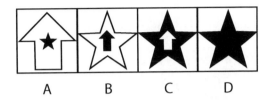

    A   B   C   D

Answer

Question 7

Work out the codes for the figures and decide which answer has the correct code for Figure 4.

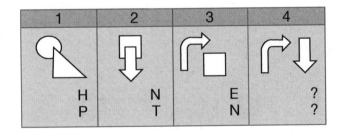

A	B	C	D
P	H	N	E
E	T	T	T

Answer

Question 8

Work out which 3D shapes from the answer options are needed to create the Question Figure.

Question Figure

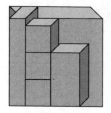

Answer Figures

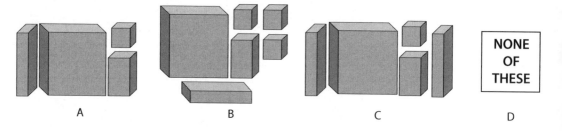

| A | B | C | D |

Answer [ ]

Question 9

Which figure is an exact rotation of the first?

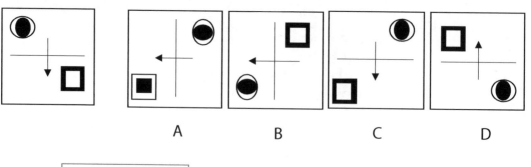

| A | B | C | D |

Answer [ ]

Question 10

Which group of shapes can be assembled to make the shape shown?

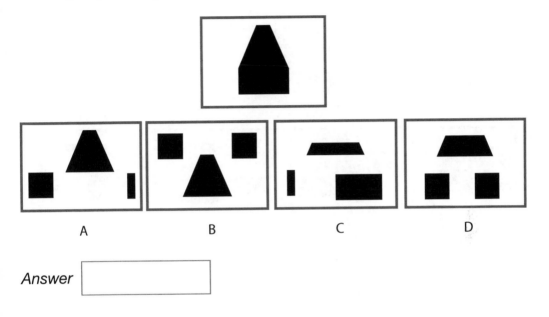

A   B   C   D

Answer

Question 11

Which group of shapes can be assembled to make the shape shown?

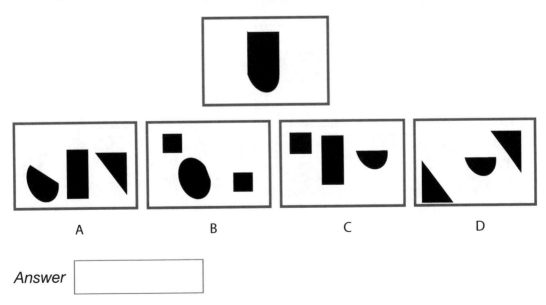

A   B   C   D

Answer

Question 12

Which group of shapes can be assembled to make the shape shown?

   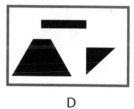

A	B	C	D

Answer

Question 13

Which group of shapes can be assembled to make the shape shown?

   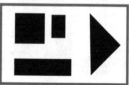

A	B	C	D

Answer

Question 14

Which group of shapes can be assembled to make the shape shown?

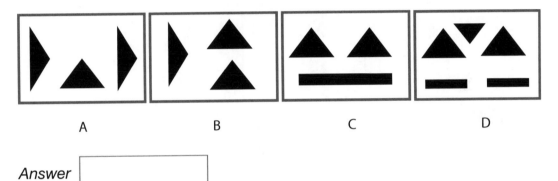

A   B   C   D

Answer

Question 15

Which SET does the TEST SHAPE belong to? (A, B or neither)

SET A	SET B	TEST SHAPE

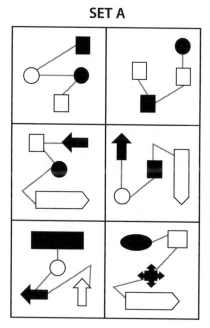 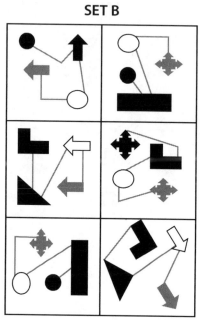 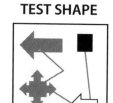

Answer [   ]

Question 16

Which SET does the TEST SHAPE belong to? (A, B or neither)

SET A	SET B	TEST SHAPE

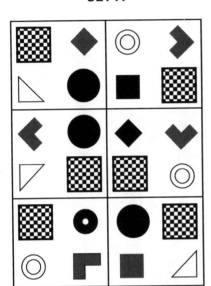  

Answer

Question 17

Which SET does the TEST SHAPE belong to? (A, B or neither).

SET A	SET B	TEST SHAPE

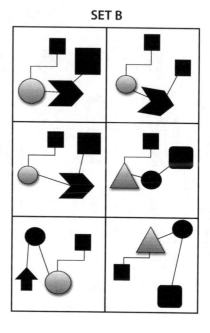

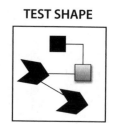

Answer

Question 18

Which SET does the TEST SHAPE belong to? (A, B or neither)

SET A	SET B	TEST SHAPE

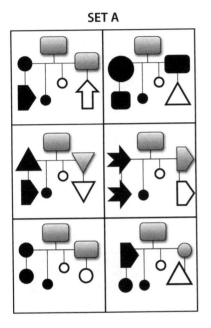 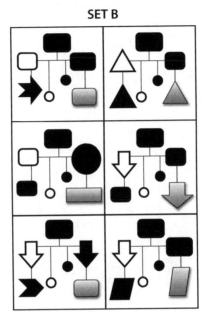 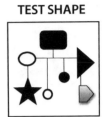

Answer

Question 19

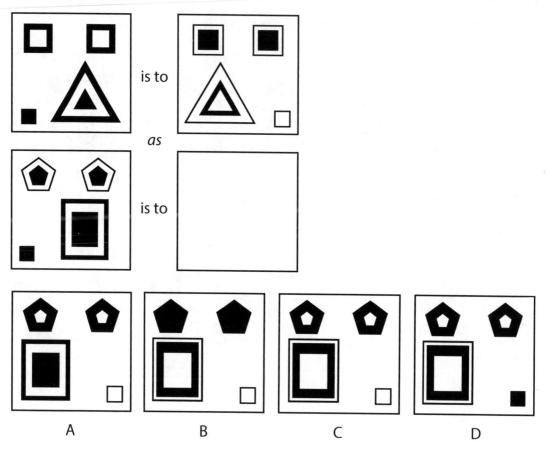

is to

as

is to

| A | B | C | D |

Answer

Question 20

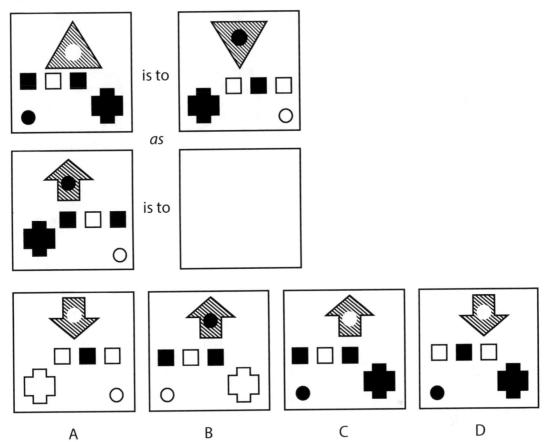

A   B   C   D

Answer

Question 21

Work out which two shapes are identical. (No rotation or reflection needed). TWO answers required.

A	B	C	D	E

Answer

Question 22

Which figure comes next in the sequence?

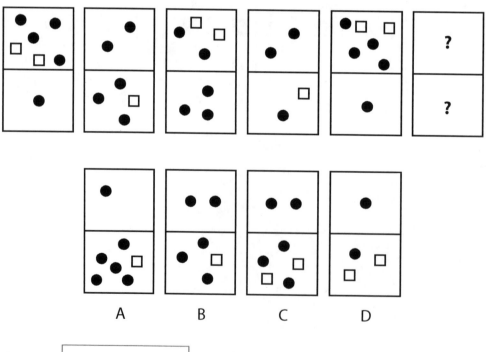

Answer

Question 23

Work out the codes for the figures and decide which answer has the correct code for Figure 4.

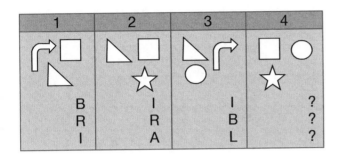

A	B	C	D
I	R	R	B
R	L	L	R
A	A	I	L

Answer [   ]

Question 24

Work out which option is a reflection of the Question Figure.

Question figure

Answer figures

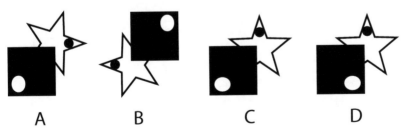

| A | B | C | D |

Answer [   ]

Question 25

Work out which of the cubes can be made from the net.

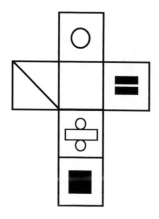

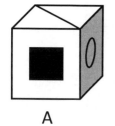

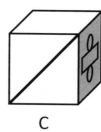
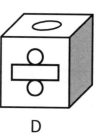

A   B   C   D

Answer [   ]

ANSWERS TO SECTION 2

Q1. B

EXPLANATION = if you look at the relationship between the first shape and the second shape, you will notice that the large hexagon changes into a small hexagon with a vertical line positioned down the middle of the shape. Therefore the large trapezoid needs to change to a small trapezoid with a vertical line positioned down the middle of the shape.

Q2. B

EXPLANATION = answer option B is correct. The triangle is rotating 90° anti-clockwise as the sequence progresses. The arrows rotate 90° clockwise as the sequence progresses. The arrows remain on the right side of the triangle.

Q3. C

EXPLANATION = as you can see in the first row of diagrams, the shapes are rotating 90° anti-clockwise. Therefore, the next shape in the sequence needs to be rotated 90° from the last diagram in the sequence.

Q4. B

EXPLANATION = in the sequence, 1 arrow is added to each diagram as the sequence progresses. Therefore, the only answer option that works is answer option B.

Q5. D

EXPLANATION = the Question Figure contains an 'L' 3D shape, 2 cuboids the same length, and a cube.

Q6. C

EXPLANATION = the sequence is as follows: the middle vertical box takes the shapes from the first row and swaps them around. For example, box 1 contains a triangle inside a square which turns into a square inside a triangle. The colour pattern changes from white on the outside and black on the inside, to black on the outside and white on the inside and vice versa. Therefore the missing box needs to contain a white arrow inside a black star.

Q7. D

EXPLANATION = the circle appears once and is coded 'H'. A triangle appears once and is coded 'P'. An arrow pointing around to the right appears twice and is coded 'E'. An arrow pointing down appears twice and is coded 'T'. A square appears twice and is coded 'N'. Therefore Figure 4 needs the code of an arrow pointing to the right (which is 'E') and an arrow pointing downwards (which is 'T').

Q8. B

EXPLANATION = the Question Figure contains 1 large 'slim' cuboid, 3 cubes, and 2 cuboids (different sizes to one another).

Q9. D

EXPLANATION = only one of the figures is an exact rotation of the first – the others are reflections or slightly modified in some way.

Q10. B

EXPLANATION = only answer option B contains the correct shapes in order to make the shape that is shown.

Q11. D

EXPLANATION = only answer option D contains the correct shapes in order to make the shape that is shown.

Q12. B

EXPLANATION = only answer option B contains the correct shapes in order to make the shape that is shown.

Q13. C

EXPLANATION = only answer option C contains the correct shapes in order to make the shape that is shown.

Q14. A

EXPLANATION = only answer option A contains the correct shapes in order to make the shape that is shown.

Q15. Neither

EXPLANATION = the test shape does not fit in to either sets. This is because the test shape has two grey shapes, which does not follow the pattern in either set.

Q16. Set A

EXPLANATION = the test shape fits in to Set A. This is because in set A each square contains a black shape, a white shape, a chequered shape and a grey shape. This is the same as the test shape.

Q17. Set B

EXPLANATION = the test shape fits in to Set B. Set B starts with a black shape, which is linked to a grey shape, to a black shape, to a black shape. The test shape follows the same pattern.

Q18. Set B

EXPLANATION = the test shape fits in to Set B. Set B starts with a black shape. The row below then follows the sequence white and black. The bottom line follows the sequence black, white, black and grey.

Q19. C

EXPLANATION = within the first diagram, the top black squares have an inner white square, which in the next diagram becomes a white square with a black inner square. The triangle alternates between black, white, black;

which changes in the next diagram to white, black, white. In the bottom left corner, there is a black square which changes to a white square in the bottom right corner.

Q20. D

EXPLANATION = within the first diagram, there is a striped triangle with a white inner circle. This changes to a striped downward pointing triangle with a black inner circle. The black cross in the bottom right corner, moves to the bottom left corner. The black dot in the bottom left corner changes to a white dot in the bottom right corner. The three horizontal squares slightly to the left with the colour pattern black, white, black, are moved slightly to the right side and have the colour pattern white, black, white.

So, the diagram you are trying to work out has to follow this format. The striped arrow with the black inner dot becomes a striped downwards pointing arrow with a white inner dot. The cross moves from the left hand side, to the right hand side but remains the same colour. The white dot at the bottom right corner becomes a black dot in the bottom left corner. The horizontal squares move to the right and have the colour pattern white, black, white etc.

Q21. A and E

EXPLANATION = none of the other shapes are identical. Figures A and E are identical.

Q22. B

EXPLANATION = the number of dots starts off as 4 in the top of the first rectangle and 1 in the bottom. The number of squares in the top of the first rectangle is 2 and 0 in the bottom. As the sequence progresses, starting from the top of the first rectangle and in alternating sections, the dots decrease by 1 each time. Once it gets to 1, the pattern starts again with 4 dots. The white squares alternate between 2 and 1 in the alternating sections of the rectangle.

Starting at the bottom of the first rectangle, you will notice there is one dot. The pattern in alternating sections of each rectangle adds one dot each time, until it reaches 3. It then works from 3 back down to 1.

Q23. B

EXPLANATION = the white arrow appears in two boxes and is coded 'B'. The white square appears in three boxes and is coded 'R'. The white triangle appears three times and is coded 'I'. The white circle appears twice and is coded 'L'. The white star appears twice and is coded 'A'. Therefore Figure 4 needs the code of a square (which is 'R'), a circle (which is 'L') and a star (which is 'A').

Q24. C

EXPLANATION = Figures A and B are rotations not reflections, so both of these answer options can be ruled out. Figure D is a reflection, but the white circle is on the wrong side of the square (it should be on the bottom left hand side of the square, not the bottom right). Figure C is an exact reflection of the Question Figure.

Q25. C

EXPLANATION = Figure A can be ruled out because the line on the top should be the 'equals' sign. Figure B can be ruled out because the side with the line on should have a circle instead. Figure D can be ruled out because there needs to be a space between the 'divide' sign and the circle.

THE
REVISION
SERIES

NON-VERBAL REASONING

(SECTION 3)

Question 1

Which two shapes are identical to one another?

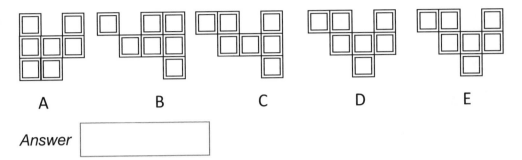

A   B   C   D   E

Answer

Question 2

Which two shapes are identical to one another?

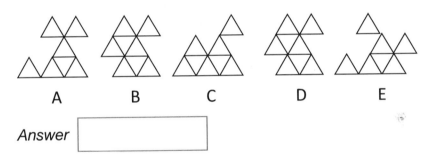

A   B   C   D   E

Answer

Question 3

Which two shapes are identical to one another?

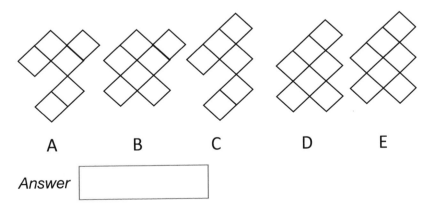

A   B   C   D   E

Answer

Question 4

Which Answer Figure is a rotation of the Question Figure?

Question figure

Answer figures

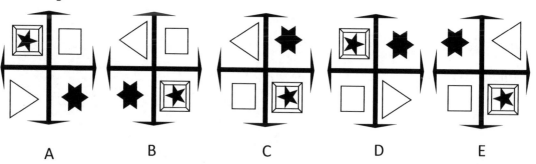

| A | B | C | D | E |

Answer

Question 5

Which Answer Figure is a rotation of the Question Figure?

Question figure

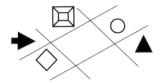

Answer figures

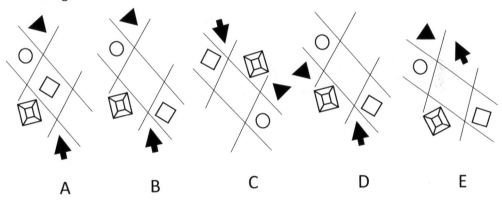

| A | B | C | D | E |

Answer

Question 6

Which of the following answers completes the sequence?

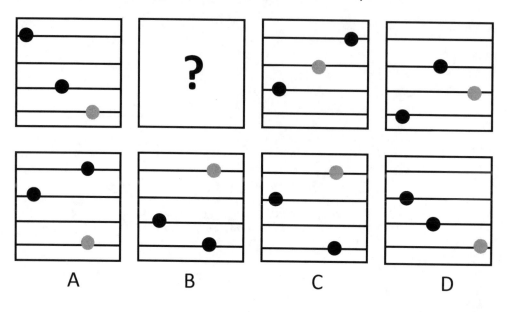

Answer

Question 7

Which Answer Figure is a rotation of the Question Figure?

Question figure

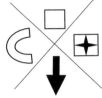

Answer figures

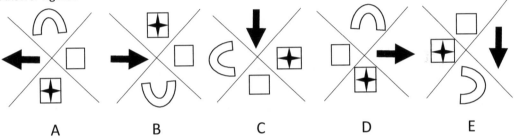

| A | B | C | D | E |

Answer

Question 8

Which shape can be created by matching the corresponding letters in the grey box?

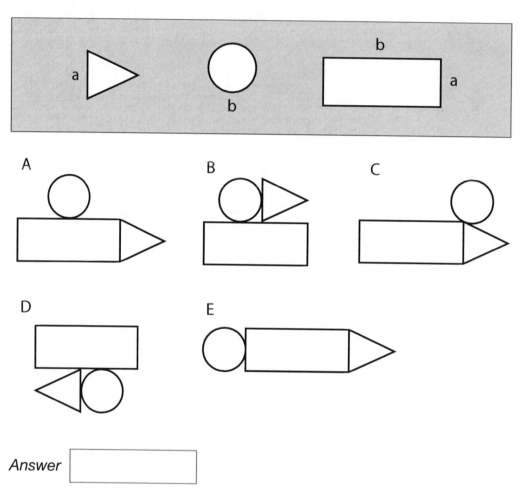

Answer

Question 9

Which shape can be created by matching the corresponding letters in the grey box?

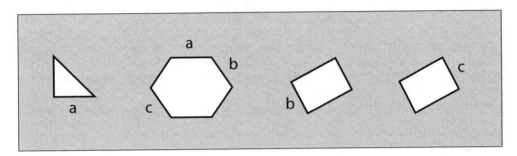

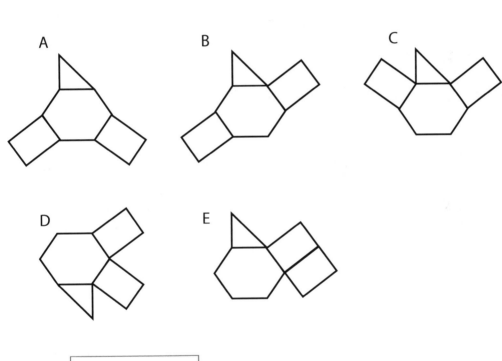

Answer

Question 10

Which of the following answers is a vertical reflection of the first shape?

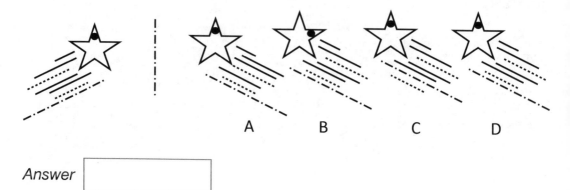

Answer [   ]

Question 11

Work out which option (A, B, C or D) would NOT look like the Question Figure if rotated.

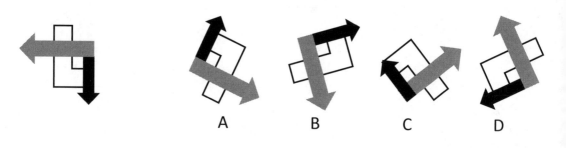

Answer [   ]

Question 12

Work out which of the cubes can be made from the net.

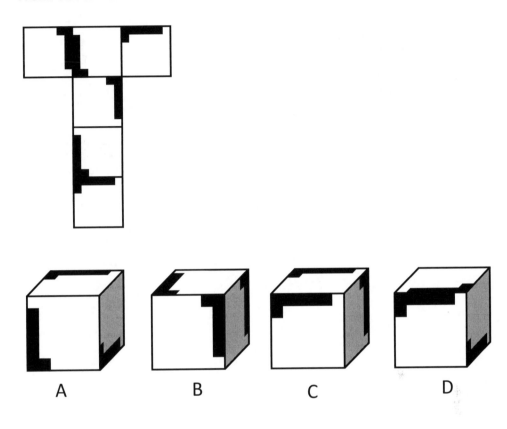

A   B   C   D

Answer

Question 13

Which shapes in Group 1 match the shapes G, J, O, R and Y in Group 2?

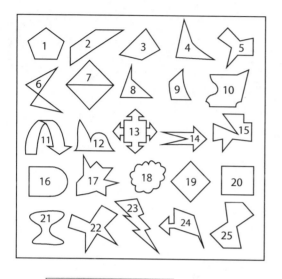

G =

J =

O =

R =

Y =

Question 14

Work out which figure (A, B, C or D) is the odd one out.

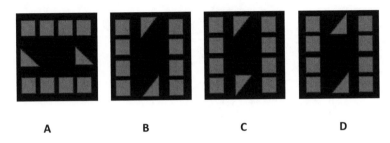

A   B   C   D

Answer

Question 15

Which shapes in Group 1 match the shapes G, H, L, T and V in Group 2?

G =

H =

L =

T =

V =

Question 16

Fill in the missing square in order to complete the grid.

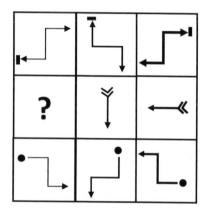

A   B   C   D

Answer

Question 17

Which shapes in Group 1 match the shapes B, F, M, P and R in Group 2?

B =

F =

M =

P =

R =

Question 18

Which shape can be created by matching the corresponding letters in the box?

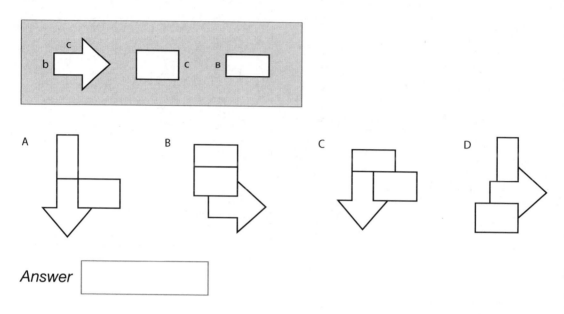

Answer

Question 19

Which shape can be created by matching the corresponding letters in the grey box?

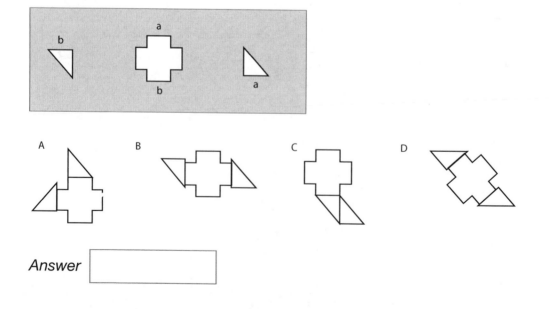

Answer

Question 20

Work out which two shapes are identical. (No rotation or reflection needed). TWO answers required.

| A | B | C | D | E |

Answer

Question 21

Work out which figure (A, B, C, D or E) is the odd one out.

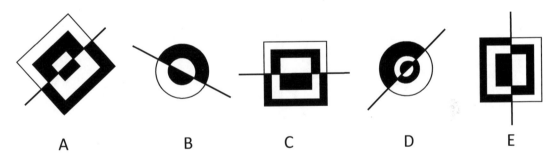

| A | B | C | D | E |

Answer

Question 22

Work out which figure (A, B, C, D or E) is the odd one out.

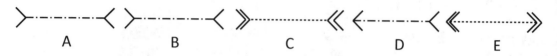

A   B   C   D   E

Answer

Question 23

Work out which figure (A, B, C or D) is the odd one out.

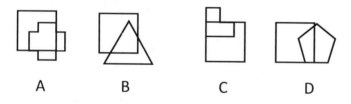

A   B   C   D

Answer

Question 24

Which shapes in Group 1 match the shapes C, E, J, K and V in Group 2?

C =

E =

J =

K =

V =

Question 25

Which of the following figures is the odd one out?

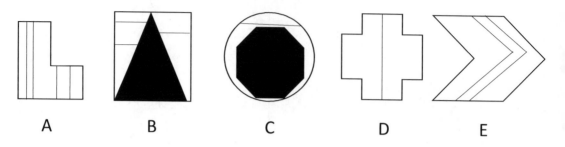

| A | B | C | D | E |

Answer [   ]

ANSWERS TO SECTION 3

Q1. D and E

EXPLANATION = only answer options D and E are identical. No other answer option is identical.

Q2. B and D

EXPLANATION = only answer options B and D are identical. No other answer option is identical.

Q3. D and E

EXPLANATION = only answer options D and E are identical. No other answer option is identical.

Q4. C

EXPLANATION = only answer option C is an exact rotation of the question figure.

Q5. B

EXPLANATION = only answer option B is an exact rotation of the question figure.

Q6. C

EXPLANATION = the sequence follows: black dot on a line, line, black dot on a line, grey dot on a line. As the sequence progresses, the dots move down one line each time, once the dot reaches the bottom it goes back to the top.

Q7. A

EXPLANATION = only answer option A is an exact rotation of the question figure.

Q8. A

EXPLANATION = if you connected all the shapes using the corresponding letters, you would get answer A.

Q9. B

EXPLANATION = if you connected all the shapes using the corresponding letters, you would get answer B.

Q10. D

EXPLANATION = Figure A can be ruled out because the thick black line and the dotted line are in the wrong place. Figure B can be ruled out because the black dot is in the wrong place. Figure C can be ruled out because the lines have all been moved around. Therefore the correct answer is Figure D.

Q11. C

Figure C is not a rotation of the Question Figure. The black arrow has been moved and has been placed on top of the grey arrow. These arrows should not be overlapping. Therefore, Figure C does not look like the Question Figure.

Q12. B

EXPLANATION = Figure A can be ruled out because the front of the cube would have to have the 'L' shape in the top right corner. Figure C can be ruled out because the top of the cube would need to have the 'L' shape in the bottom left corner. Figure D can be ruled out because the 'L' shape on the right hand side of the cube would need to be in the top right corner.

Q13. G=18, J=6, O=17, R=15, Y=1

Q14. B

Figure B is the only one where the two small triangles in the centre face opposite ways.

Q15. G=17, H=18, L=24, T=9, V=8

Q16. D

EXPLANATION = in each row, the shape is rotated 90° clockwise each time. The shapes also get wider (darker) as the sequence progresses. In order to work out the missing square, you need to select the thinnest arrow and then work back 90° anti-clockwise from box 2.

Q17. B=6, F=16, M=15, P=22, R=25

Q18. A

EXPLANATION = figure A is the correct answer. After placing the shapes together, all the shapes are in the correct position if you rotate the entire shape 90° clockwise.

Q19. D

EXPLANATION = figure D is the correct answer. After placing the shapes together, all the shapes are in the correct position if you rotate the entire shape 45° anti-clockwise.

Q20. A and C

EXPLANATION = none of the other figures are identical. Figures A and C are identical.

Q21. B

EXPLANATION = Figure B is the odd one out because all the other shapes have the same alternating pattern, consisting of three shapes inside the overall shape. Figure B only has two shapes inside the overall shape.

Q22. D

EXPLANATION = Figure D is the odd one out because all the other figures have arrows pointing in different directions, whereas Figure D has the arrows pointing both to the left.

Q23. A

EXPLANATION = all the other figures use the two large shapes to create an overlapped shape which has four sides.

Q24. C=9, E=12, J=19, K=18, V=4

Q25. D

EXPLANATION = figure D is the odd one out because all of the other figures contain shapes in which the sides all add up to 10. For example, in Figure A, it contains an 'L' shape (which contains 6 sides) and has 4 vertical lines inside the shape.

THE
REVISION
SERIES

ANSWERING
YOUR
QUESTIONS

You have now reached the end of your Kent Test booklet for Non-Verbal Reasoning. You should now feel confident enough to tackle any Non-Verbal Reasoning question that you will encounter. Before you go, we recommend that you read through our final top tips on how to answer the questions. You can use these tips in practice, and in your assessment.

Remember, for each exam in the Kent Test, you will be provided with a testing booklet and an answer booklet. These will be similar to the following:

- Maths and English Testing Booklet;
- Maths and English Answer Sheet;
- Reasoning Testing Booklet;
- Reasoning Answer Sheet.

You need to read the questions in the testing booklet and choose the correct answer, which you <u>MUST</u> then write on the answer sheet provided. When you take the Kent Test, only the answers written on the answer sheet will be marked. Any other written work or rough drafts, will not be marked.

Make sure that at the start of your Kent Test, you take the time to read through the set of instructions on the front of your examination booklet. This will tell you everything you need to know regarding the Kent Test, including how to use the answer booklet and where to write your answers.

- Make sure that you mark your chosen answer for the corresponding question number. For example, if you answered question 5, make sure that you mark the answer for question 5!

- Any rough work, drafts or calculations should not be written on the answer sheet. Instead you can ask for extra sheets of paper or write them in your testing booklet. (Any additional paper or the testing booklet will not be marked!)

Example Answer Sheet

Here is a basic example marking sheet which gives you some indication of what you can expect in your assessment. For example, if you chose answer option 'D' as the correct answer for question 1 on the Non-Verbal test, you would mark a line in pencil or pen, horizontally through the box (as shown).

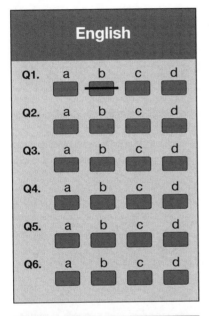

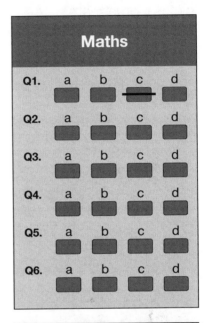

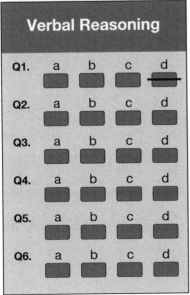

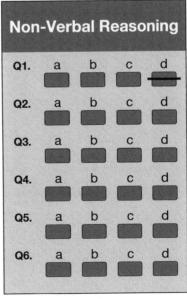

Good luck with your 11+ Kent Test, Non-Verbal Reasoning. We wish you the very best of luck with all your future endeavours!

The how2become team

The How2Become team

WANT MORE HELP WITH THE KENT TEST?

CHECK OUT OUR OTHER KENT TEST GUIDES:

How2Become have created other FANTASTIC guides to help you and your child learn all they need to pass the Kent Test.

There are 100s of practice questions within these guides all with detailed explanations. These guides also include expert insider tips and advice to help you or your child feel at ease on exam day.

FOR MORE INFORMATION ON OUR KENT TEST WORKBOOKS, PLEASE CHECK OUT THE FOLLOWING:

WWW.HOW2BECOME.COM

Get Access To
FREE
Educational Practice Papers
(KS2, 11+, KS3, GCSE)

www.MyEducationalTests.co.uk